First Facts

The Magna Carta

by Marcia Amidon Lusted

PEBBLE
a capstone imprint

First Facts are published by Pebble
1710 Roe Crest Drive, North Mankato, Minnesota 56003.
www.mycapstone.com

Library of Congress Cataloging-in-Publication Data
Names: Lusted, Marcia Amidon, author.
Title: The Magna Carta / by Marcia Amidon Lusted.
Description: North Mankato, Minnesota : Capstone, [2020]
Identifiers: LCCN 2019004126| ISBN 9781977109156 (hardcover)
ISBN 9781977110145 (pbk.) | ISBN 9781977109170 (ebook pdf)
Subjects: LCSH: Magna Carta—Juvenile literature. | Constitutional history—England—Juvenile literature. | Constitutional history—United States—Sources—Juvenile literature. | United States. Constitution. 1st–10th Amendments—Juvenile literature.
Classification: LCC KD3946 .L87 2019 | DDC 342.4202/9—dc23
LC record available at https://lccn.loc.gov/2019004126

Editorial Credits
Alesha Sullivan, editor; Elyse White, designer; Jo Miller, media researcher; Katy LaVigne, production specialist

Image Credits
Alamy: Heritage Image Partnership Ltd, 12; Library of Congress, Cover (bottom), 9; Newscom: British Library/Album, 19, Heritage Images/London Metropolitan Archive/City of London, 15, Heritage Images/The Print Collector, 5, 13, World History Archive, 6, 11; Shutterstock: David Smart, 7, Everett Historical, 17, Orhan Cam, 21; Wikimedia, Cover (top), 8, NARA, 20

Design Elements
Shutterstock: Scisetti Alfio

Printed and bound in China.
1671

Table of Contents

Chapter 1

A Charter in the Making

King John of England was not happy. It was June 15, 1215, and he had to sign an important document. It was called the Magna Carta. It was going to make sure that the people of England had **rights**. The king could no longer do whatever he wanted.

Fact:

The name *Magna Carta* is Latin for "great charter." A charter is a legal document.

King John of England

right—something the law allows people to do, such as the right to vote or the right to speak freely

The people of England did not think King John was a good king. He made them pay high **taxes**. He took food from farmers without paying for it. The people wanted **justice.**

Important men called barons told the king that he must sign a document. It said the king had to stop his unfair actions. This document would become the Magna Carta.

Power and Greed

King John wanted control of the city of London, England, because it was a very rich city. People paid high taxes that went directly to the king. The barons took control of London in 1215. They kept control until King John agreed to sign the Magna Carta.

The Magna Carta was written to help protect the rights of England's people.

justice—fair behavior or treatment

tax—money that people or businesses must give to the government to pay for what the government does

Chapter 2

Writing the Magna Carta

King John met with the barons at a place called Runnymede in England. They argued about the document for four days. They made changes to it. Finally, the king agreed. He signed the Magna Carta. He promised that he would treat the people fairly.

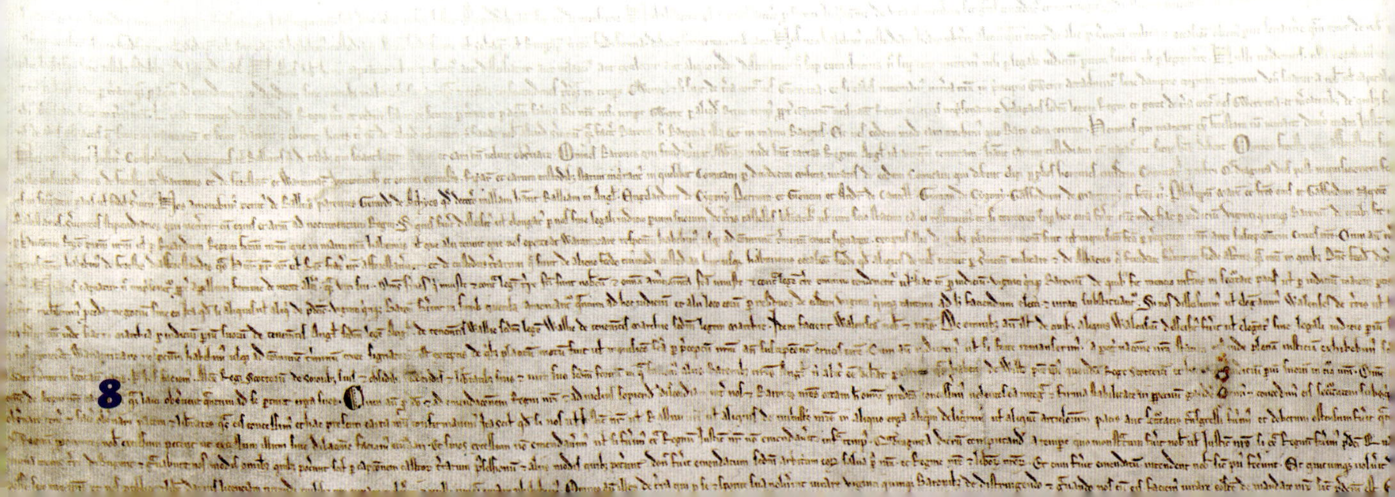

King John signed the Magna Carta and agreed to be fairer with the people of England.

The Magna Carta was the first written **constitution** in all of Europe. The document would later help England form a **democracy**.

The Magna Carta was important to England for many reasons. It made sure the people had rights. It limited the powers of kings and queens.

Fact:

The Magna Carta was written in the Latin language. At the time, many legal documents for governments and churches were written in Latin.

After the Magna Carta was signed, all the kings and queens of England had to agree to its rules.

constitution—a written system of laws in a country that state the rights of people and the powers of government

democracy—a kind of government in which the people make decisions by voting

Chapter 3

A Civil War

Instead of war, the Magna Carta was supposed to be a **treaty** for peace. But King John did not keep his promises. The king demanded money from the barons to pay for his war with France. But the barons did not want to pay. They were ready to stand up to King John.

The barons decided to rise up against King John after the king would not listen to their wishes.

treaty—a formal agreement between groups

The barons fought back. A **civil war** began. It became known as the First Barons' War. King John became ill during the First Barons' War. He died in 1216, ending the war.

After King John died, his son Henry III became king. He took out some of the **clauses** in the Magna Carta. This helped keep peace between the people and the **government**.

civil war—a war between opposing groups within one country

clause—a section of a legal document

government—the group of people who make laws, rules, and decisions for a country or state

After King John's death, King Henry III changed parts of the Magna Carta. He wanted to make the people happy.

Chapter 4

Across the Ocean

In the 1600s, a group of people left England and moved to North America. They formed a colony. Leaders of the **colony** later decided they wanted to make their own laws and government. They wrote the Declaration of Independence. They broke free from Great Britain's rule.

The Magna Carta and the Declaration of Independence are similar. Both documents say that people have rights and **freedoms**.

When America's colonies wanted to break free from Great Britain, leaders thought of the Magna Carta. American people wanted rights. They wanted rules for the government to follow.

colony—an area that has been settled by people from another country, typically ruled by another country

freedom—the right to live the way you want

Part of the Magna Carta is called the Habeas Corpus act. Habeas Corpus is a law that says people can't be put in jail unlawfully. This means if you are in jail, you have the right to be seen by a judge in court. The judge will decide if, by law, you should stay in jail or be let go. Today Habeas Corpus is an important part of the U.S. legal system.

the Magna Carta

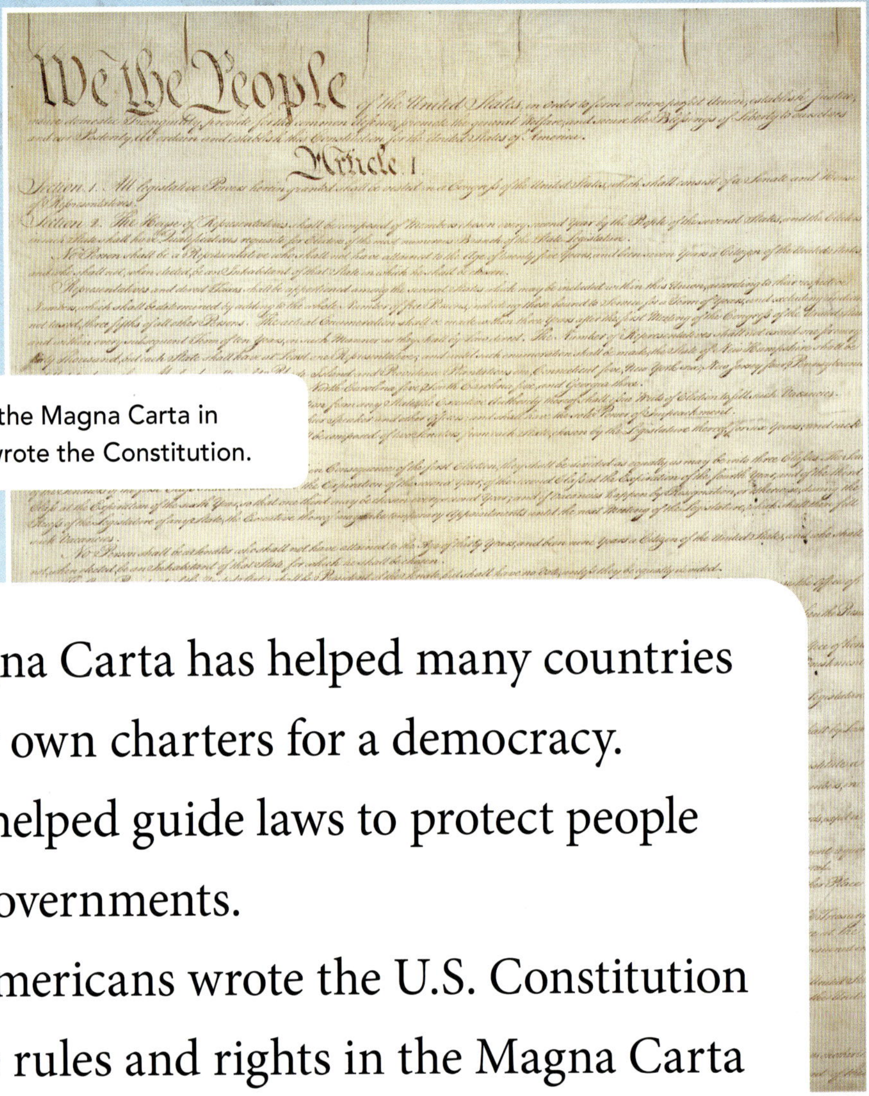

U.S. leaders kept the Magna Carta in mind when they wrote the Constitution.

The Magna Carta has helped many countries create their own charters for a democracy. It has also helped guide laws to protect people and their governments.

When Americans wrote the U.S. Constitution in 1787, the rules and rights in the Magna Carta came to mind. The Magna Carta helped shape the U.S. government into what it is today.

The National Archives in the U.S. capital is home to many important documents.

Fact:

A copy of the Magna Carta is on display at the National Archives Museum in Washington, D.C.

Glossary

civil war (SI-vil WOR)—a war between opposing groups within one country

clause (KLAWZ)—a section of a legal document

colony (KAH-luh-nee)—an area that has been settled by people from another country, typically ruled by another country

constitution (kahn-stuh-TOO-shuhn)—a written system of laws in a country that state the rights of people and the powers of government

democracy (di-MAH-kruh-see)—a kind of government in which the people make decisions by voting

freedom (FREE-duhm)—the right to live the way you want

government (GUHV-urn-muhnt)—the group of people who make laws, rules, and decisions for a country or state

justice (JUHSS-tiss)—fair behavior or treatment

right (RITE)—something the law allows people to do, such as the right to vote or the right to speak freely

tax (TAKS)—money that people or businesses must give to the government to pay for what the government does

treaty (TREE-tee)—a formal agreement between groups

Read More

Barrington, Richard. *The Magna Carta*. Let's Find Out! New York: Rosen Publishing, 2017.

Cameron, Eileen. *Rupert's Parchment: Story of Magna Carta*. Herndon, VA: Mascot Books, 2015.

Spier, Peter. *We the People: The Constitution of the United States*. New York: Doubleday Books, 2014.

Internet Sites

King John and the Magna Carta
https://www.bbc.com/bitesize/guides/zqgqtfr/revision/1

Magna Carta Today
https://www.bl.uk/magna-carta/themes/magna-carta-today

Critical Thinking Questions

1. In what ways did King John treat the people of England unfairly?
2. How did the Magna Carta help England form a democracy?
3. The Magna Carta is an important part of England's history. Why was it also important to other places in the world?

Index